# NOT MOMS

*A Guidebook*

## HOW TO SURVIVE WITH ALL THAT EXTRA TIME AND MONEY

By **Julie Wittner** and **Katie Von Till**

Illustrations by **Matthew Patrick Davis**

# DEDICATION

**We dedicate this book to you. You deserve it.**

# TABLE OF CONTENTS

ACKNOWLEDGMENTS

Our sincerest thanks:

Jeff LaPensee - you make everything better.

Our NOT MOMS friends who shared their childfree thoughts with us.

The moms out there who are doing the hard work so we don't have to.

Our moms.

# HELLO, FELLOW NOT MOMS!
## (AND ALL CHILDFREE PEOPLE!)

Do you sometimes wonder if deciding to be childfree was the right choice for you?

Does that choice make you feel isolated at times, or make it difficult to relate to your friends with kids?

Do you find yourself constantly having to defend your choice to your dental hygienist?

Us, too! But we, the authors of this book, are excited to tell you that you have made a SPECTACULAR life choice!

Even though your family, your friends, your religion, and your government may not approve, we have come to the conclusion that, like us, you shouldn't give a fuck.

Others don't need to understand our choices. It would be great if they did, but we've learned to take pride in the fact that breeders think we're bizarre. We embrace being outside the norm. We are following in the footsteps of other childfree greats. Like Oprah. That's right. We are OPRAH.

Kidding. We are not Oprah. We are Katie and Julie, and we are NOT MOMS.

## And so are you!

# SEXY STATISTICS ABOUT THE CHILDFREE!

According to a recent survey by the U.S. Census Bureau, 52% of women in their childbearing years have not had children.

Time Magazine published a survey showing that 80% of women and men state they could lead fulfilling lives without having children. We  didn't make that up! The scientists did.

# "WAIT … YOU DON'T LIKE KIDS?"

Actually, we love kids!

Other people's kids. Some of them are gosh darn adorable. They're incredibly funny and sweet. In fact, they are so darling that they make you want to have kids. It's very manipulative. If anyone is the culprit for making you feel bad about not having kids, it's kids. That's how they getcha!

Stop feeling bad about not having kids. We don't have to defend our position (but in case you do want to defend it: financial hardships, world overpopulation, episiotomies).

Instead, let's embrace and celebrate our choices!

Through careful diagnostic life experience and double-blind testing*, we've uncovered the secrets to living one's best and most joyous childfree life. And we are so excited to share our findings, musings, and helpful tips with you. And so, we give you ...

NOT MOMS: A Guidebook — How to Survive With All That Extra Time and Money.

*No animals were harmed during testing. Also, there was no testing.*

Testy the Bunny says:
This book is 100%
CRUELTY FREE!

# CHAPTER 1

# SELFISH OR SELFLESS?

Is your decision to forgo having kids selfish or selfless?

Let's discuss.

Adding to the world's population is bad for the environment. We didn't make that up. Researchers did!

You're a busy childfree person trying to earn the Nobel Peace Prize/ end world hunger/ figure out which bin your disposable coffee cup goes into. You are taking care of the earth. Earth is your baby. If you look away for one fucking second, earth ends up on the pole getting dollar bills shoved into her g-string.

You are taking care
of the earth.
Earth is your baby.

Some say the human race will be in trouble if there aren't enough babies being born to support our aging population. We say, "Aren't the robots going to take over eventually anyhow?" Make up your minds, Doomsday People!

Look. We love kids. But having kids is a crapshoot. Sure, you could spend hundreds of thousands of dollars and end up raising the president of the United States. But on the flip side, you could spend hundreds of thousands of dollars and end up raising that *other* president of the United States. Yikes! It's risky. So we say, "If you don't play, you can't lose!"

So ... selfish or selfless?

**ANSWER: SELFLESS**

# THE TALK - TELLING YOUR LOVED ONES YOU AREN'T PROCREATING

Breaking the news to your loved ones can be a tricky endeavor. Use the following suggestions to break the ice.

### <u>YOUR PARENTS</u>

- Great steaks, dad! I'm not having kids. Pass the potatoes, please.

- Mom, I left my retainer on the school bus nine times. You and I both know I'm not up to the challenge of parenthood.

- Remember when I was 17 and you told me that if I got pregnant it would ruin my life? Yeah, that.

- Uncle Tim never had kids, and he lives all by himself in a basement flat in Brooklyn! I mean, WOW!

## LOVE INTERESTS

- Nice to meet you. No to kids. Amirite?

- I love you so much that I don't want kids with you. You're welcome.

- DINKFY. (Dual Income No Kids Fuck Yeah)

- I like having sex with you. Why put an end to that?

- It's a shame more kids aren't dogs.

- Tonight, for kicks, let's get up every two hours and take turns blowing an air horn in each other's ears. Sound fun? No? Agreed.

# CHAPTER 3

# "ARE YOU HAVING KIDS?" AND OTHER STUPID QUESTIONS

For some reason people feel compelled to know what you're going to do with your ova/semen. We think it's because they're trying to figure out what to do with *their* ova/semen. Or maybe they just want to distract you and steal your wallet. Either way, say something weird when answering this line of questioning. Because why not make them feel as uncomfortable as they are making you feel? Plus, it's fun!

The following are some of our favorite answers to the question ...

"ARE YOU HAVING KIDS?"

- Am I having them do what?

- We can't. We own a recliner made of swords.

- We can't have kids. We both love Cheez Whiz and we don't want to pass that trait down.

- So nice of you to ask! Thank you. I'm good with this. (Hold up your sandwich.)

- Fuck no. I mean, yours are great. Ours would be terrible. They'd be gorgeous, but terrible.

- "We decided not to have kids because... well... (*point to their kids*). No offense."

- We wanted kids, but we also wanted to have sex on the kitchen counter. So, kids were not really an option for us.

- We can't have kids. Our building frowns upon it: No Dogs. No Kids.

- We tried. But not that hard.

# CHAPTER 4

## FREEDOM!

Yay you. You have so much freedom.

How awesome is it to be able to bring home whatever you want and not have to worry about a child being injured, emotionally scarred, or killed by those things?

For example: Poison, medication, electrical sockets, chainsaws, random people you pick up at bars.

So cool, right?! In addition, you can leave "not safe for children" items out in plain sight on your coffee table!

Such as: Alcohol, knives, nude photos, popcorn, things made out of glass, porcupines, boiling water, lit candles, drugs, candy, swords, q-tips, marbles, sharp sticks, fire, cell phones, whole grapes, turpentine, peanut butter, and cocaine. And all on a sharp-cornered coffee table.

# NOT-SAFE-FOR-CHILDREN ITEMS
## YOU MAY FREELY ENJOY *(partial list):*

1. Fire pit

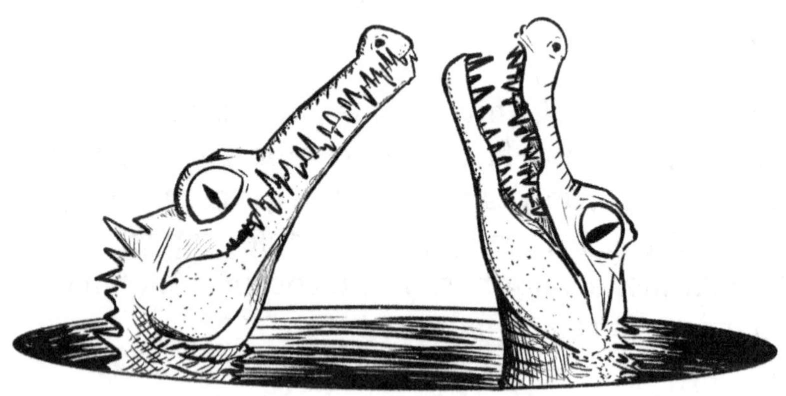

2. Alligator pit

3. Chainsaw

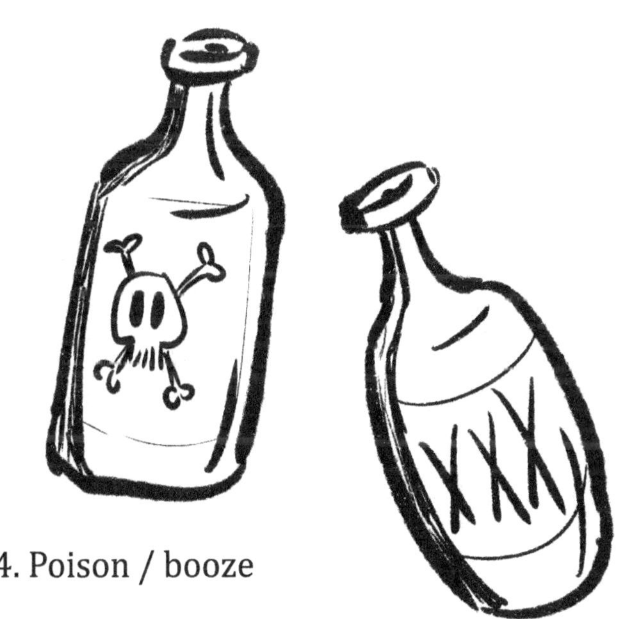

4. Poison / booze

5. Light socket with butter knife

6. Various explosives

7. Choking hazards

8. Spear

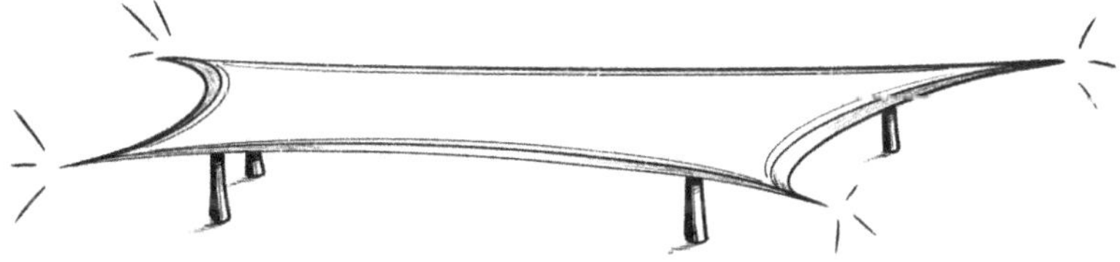

9. Coffee table *(extra sharp corners!)*

How fun is that? Your life is fucking fantastic!

Now go smoke a doobie while you make a last-minute dinner reservation at your favorite restaurant for you and your favorite childfree dinner companion.

But first, be sure to take a long cat nap with your cat.

Why?

Because you can!

Why?

**BECAUSE YOU HAVE ...**

FREEDOM!
FREEDOM!
FREEDOM!
FREEDOM!
FREEDOM!
FREEDOM!
FREEDOM!
FREEDOM!
FREEDOM!
FREEDOM!
FREEDOM!

# <u>WHAT TO DO WITH YOUR</u><br>**<u>EXTRA TIME</u>**

- Sleep when all your friends' babies sleep.

- Win a gold medal.

- Cure herpes.

- Learn how to make bespoke nut-butters.

- Video games.

- Run for President.

- Breed your own donkey hybrid.

- Write this book.

- Engage in a staring contest with a tortoise. Then race!

- Clean your house while playing back-to-back slasher films on TV.

- Keep your laptop open to something naughty all day. Every time you pass your laptop, engage.

- Make up and sing awesome songs about your freedom.

- Travel.

- Travel at the last minute.

- Travel internationally. (see next page)

**HOT TIP** - When traveling internationally, people will undoubtedly ask, "Do you have kids?"

Learn how to say your favorite answer in multiple languages.

<u>EXAMPLE</u>:

## "Hello. Do you have kids?"

## "We can't have kids. We both love Cheez Whiz and we don't want to pass that trait down."

## <u>TRANSLATIONS</u>

**FRENCH:** On ne peut pas avoir d'enfants. Nous aimons tous les deux le Whiz Du Fromage. Nous ne voulons pas transmettre ça.

**SPANISH:** No podemos tener hijos. A los dos nos encanta Cheez Whiz y no queremos transmitir ese rasgo.

**CANADIAN:** Sorry … sorry … excuse me … pardon … eh?

**BRITISH:** Oy. We can'ave kids. We bof love The Cheez of Whiz, love – and we don't wanna want to pass at shite down, Govn'ah.

**LATIN:** Pellentesque non possumus. Ambo amamus Cheez Whiz et nolumus transire lineamentum.

**GERMAN:** Wir können keine Kinder haben! Wir lieben Cheez Whiz und wir möchten das nicht weitervererben.

**ITALIAN:** Mamma Mia! Non possiamo avere figli. Ci piace Cheez Whiz e non vogliamo trasmettere questa caratteristica.

**PIG LATIN:** Eway antcay aveway idskay. Eway othbay ovelay Eezchay Izwhay anday eway on'tday antway otay asspay atthay aittray ownday.

**YIDDISH:** Oy Vey. Mir kenen nisht hobn kinder. Mir beyde libe Cheez Whiz aun mir ton nisht veln tsu forn dem treyt arop.

**JAPANESE:** Kodomo wo tsukuru koto ga dekimasen. Identeki no mondai mitai ... So so so, DATTE, Futari to mo "Cheez Whiz" ga daikobutsu na node kono DNA ga utsuchattara YABAI jyan-dame dame dame.

子供を作る事が出来ません。遺伝的の問題みたい、、、そそそ、だって、二人とも"チーズウィーズ"が大好物なのでこのDNAがうつちゃっらヤバイじゃん?！〜ダメダメダメ.

# WHAT TO DO WITH YOUR
# EXTRA MONEY

| DON'T BUY THIS | BUY THAT |
| --- | --- |
| Baby Bottles | Beer Bottles |
| Diapers | Sexy Underwear |
| Baby Shark Merchandise | Caviar |
| School Uniform | Sexy School Uniform |
| Tricycle | ATV |
| Barbie Doll | Blow Up Doll |
| Highchair | Massage Chair |
| Potty Seat | Bidet |
| Bath Toy Boat | Speed Boat |
| Crib | Waterbed |
| School Supplies | Botox and Fillers |
| Changing Table | Pool Table |
| Pacifier | Xanax |
| Car Seat | Sidecar |
| Booster Seat | Balenciaga Platforms |
| Teething Ring | Gummies *(where legal)* |
| Baby Powder | Cocaine |
| Rectal Thermometer | Butt Plug |
| Playpen | She Shed |
| Baby Bjorn | Cat Bjorn |
| Sandwich Bags | Designer Bags |
| Lunch Box | Box Seats |
| Bouncy House | House |

# WORDS YOU CAN SAY OUT LOUD BECAUSE YOU DON'T HAVE KIDS

You are the master of your own nasty mouth. No need to spell ANYTHING! Just run around swearing. All day long. For NO reason at all.

<h1 style="text-align:center"><u>SUGGESTED NAUGHTY WORD LIST:</u></h1>

- The F word

- The S word

- The B word

- The D word

- The other F word

- The MF word

- The S of a B word

- The T word

- The A word

- Cunt

**Wasn't that fun?**

You are a naughty, childfree rebel! By the way, even though we've given you permission to say cunt, you should NEVER say cunt. Cunt is a disgusting word. It's deplorable that the word cunt is in this book four times. Now five. Do NOT say it EVER. Unless you're in England. Then say cunt as much as you like. Darn it! That's 6 cunts.

And it's not just cuss words! You can also say this crap!

<u>SUGGESTED NAUGHTY PHRASES LIST:</u>

- Do me right now.

- I'm so drunk.

- We're getting a divorce.

- The dog is dead.

- You're my favorite.

- Let's sleep 'til noon.

- I'm going to masturbate for a few minutes. Hold my beer.

- Shut up, stupid.

- Cancel with your parents. Tell them we're sick. Massage Hut has a last minute opening for a couple's massage.

- The strippers will be here in ten minutes. Hide the coke.

- Cookies for dinner!

# CHAPTER 7

## CAREERS FOR THE CHILDFREE

You don't have kids. That's great news! You don't have to be a role model!

Follow your dreams. Follow your heart. Follow the Grateful Dead, you sexy beast!

Travel the country in a van reading night-night stories to Rock 'n' Roll groupies! Become the inventor of marshmallow prizefighting gloves. Or choose an equally frivolous career ... like Supreme Court Justice.

And by the way, parenthood is NOT the hardest job in the world. The hardest job is Alaskan crab fisherman.

# "The hardest job is Alaskan crab fisherman."

CHAPTER 8

# EXPERIENCE THE WONDERS OF LIFE AGAIN

Often parents will say, "I'm experiencing the wonders of life again through my child's eyes." We say, **"Skip the Middleman."**

Why live vicariously through a child?
**Just BE a child.**

SUGGESTIONS

- In the workplace, shoot spitballs at your boss. If you like someone, pull their hair.

- Get tattoos today that you *currently* regret.

- Fill your afternoons with numerous extracurricular activities. Get your mother to drive you and make your friend's mother pick you up.

- Get *yourself* a Swiss au pair.

- Wear your favorite superhero costume to the office. When coworkers ask if you're going to a costume party, give them the side-eye and growl, "No. I'm Batman."

"Go with your parents on all their vacations. Stay in the room with them and sleep in their bed. Stir a lot so they can't sleep."

- Make all the funny faces you want.
  (*Hint: It won't stay that way.*)

- Don't eat your vegetables.
  (*But remember, no TV if you don't.*)

- Go to the county fair with your aunt. Ask her to buy you a balloon. If she says no, throw a temper tantrum. After your second funnel cake and third deep-fried whatever, get your face painted and walk around barking like a dog. Then vomit.

- After you get a cavity (see above), tell your dentist that you've been a good patient, and you want a prize from the treasure chest. Take at least fifteen minutes to decide which toy you want.

- In your front yard, strip down to your undies and spin in circles until you fall and break your ankle.

- Put on a show in your backyard! Cast your neighbors. Make everyone in the neighborhood come over and watch. Charge five cents.

# Surprise yourself with a pony!

# CHAPTER 9

# GIVING ADVICE TO YOUR FRIENDS WITH KIDS

Look, you're not a parent, but that doesn't mean you don't have the impulses of a parent bubbling up inside you. When you see your friends fucking up their kids, you just want to help. And why shouldn't you? You're just as qualified as they are to raise their kids.

You have LEGIT real-world parent/child experience. Like the time when you were 13 and your parents found out you stole a Dr. Pepper-scented lip gloss from the local drugstore and they made you take it back and apologize to Eric, the super hot twenty-something manager, which embarrassed the crap out of you. You never did that again! That was GREAT parenting.

Or the time your mom put pot brownies in the freezer with a sign on it that read "DO NOT TOUCH," and you touched it ... again and again. That was BAD parenting. You've seen it all. Your parents fucked you up, too.

HOWEVER, be forewarned, your sister-in-law who hasn't slept in 186 days doesn't want advice from someone without kids. You are the enemy. You are rested and fully functional.

But staying silent would be a disservice, as you have so much to give in the way of objective advice. You're on the outside looking in at all of their mistakes. Parents are too close to the situation to see their own foibles.

So ... don't be silent, be *COVERT.*

Use your pets as examples to give advice.

"Oh boy. When we let Sir Nubly Bumpkins sleep between me and my husband, it took much longer to get him to spend the night in his *own* newspaper heap. Just sayin'."

Use your own parents as examples.

"It's so fun you let your kids run all over the store. My mom used to let me do that, too. This one time she wasn't paying attention, and I ended up going home with one of the nice men who offered me a ride in a choo-choo train. So fun! There was no train though, which was odd. Hmmm."

Throw other parent-friends under the bus.

"Did you hear? Tina's son was playing video games with the sound on at a restaurant. One of the other patrons got so angry that he turned into a werewolf and ATE Jordan. They are really gonna miss that kid."

# CHAPTER 10

# EXPECT THE UNEXPECTED

You wouldn't believe what some people will say TO YOUR FACE about your childbearing choices. It's very important that you brace yourself for this unsolicited feedback.

The following are things people have actually said to Katie and Julie. Don't worry, we find them mostly funny. Mostly.

> "You have such great genetics. It's a shame to waste those."
>
> *-Julie's mom*

> "I'm sad you'll never know what this love feels like."
>
> *-Julie's sister*

> "Having children is the meaning of life."
>
> *-Katie's brother*

"You don't have time. Scoot down."
*–Julie's gynecologist*

"You are the last of our family. The tree dies here. This is on you."
*-Julie's grandparents*

"Make sure if you are going to have a child, it's soon. My mother was almost 44 when I was born and well ..."
*-Katie's dad*

"Thank god you didn't have kids."
*-Everyone to Katie**

*The only time others are happy you didn't have kids is when you get divorced. Katie has been divorced twice so she would know.

# *"There's still time."*
### *-Katie's LYFT driver*

# CHAPTER 11

## THE FEAR OF MISSING OUT

Here's how it goes ...

You're walking along minding your own blissful, childfree business and then it happens ...

THE PROCREATION INDUSTRIAL COMPLEX! *(Cue scary music.)*

## COMMERCIALS

## TV SHOWS

## COUNTRY MUSIC

## SOCIAL MEDIA

## POLITICS

The **FOMO** (Fear Of Missing Out) comes hard and fast. Suddenly, your life feels meaningless and empty. Next thing you know you're crying and finishing a whole box of *(insert favorite snack here)* because you don't have the one thing that would make your life complete –

**A CHILD.**

<u>THINGS THAT MAY TRIGGER FOMO</u>
*<u>(partial list)</u>*

- Scrolling on social media #blessed

- Country music stations

- TV commercials

- Television shows about families

- Movies about families

- Families

- Well-behaved kids

- Quiet babies

- Sleeping babies

- Laughing babies

- The smell of babies

- Matching mom-daughter outfits

So, how do you compete with the baby industrial complex? What's our super fun antidote to combat your baby FOMO?

Sorry, childfree friend. There is no antidote for baby FOMO. You can't be in both clubs. No one can. **Unless time travel or multiverses.***

Yep. The bad news is you don't get to join that club. But here is the good news ... YOU DO GET TO JOIN THIS CLUB! The NOT MOMS Club.

And here's more good news ... while you are experiencing your no-child-FOMO, here's what else you're missing out on:

- Catching vomit in your hands.

- Waiting in line for Santa Claus at the mall.

- Waiting in the long line of cars at school pickup.

- Constant interruptions while watching your favorite reality TV show.

- Poopy diapers.

- Getting baby pee in your face/mouth.

- Your kid telling you that you ruin everything and they hate you!

*Read our future book from another universe, "Parenthood and Your Freedom in the Multiverse - A Guide to Having It All."*

- Cleaning up all day long after your children.

- Making eight meals a day.

- Screaming temper tantrums.

- Very little sleep for at least 2-45 years.

- Matching mom-daughter outfits.

- Baby boob bites.

# PARENTAL URGES

Look, we totally get it. We get parental urges too! It's perfectly normal.

## That's why we have cats!

*If no cats are available, you must find another way to let these parental urges out! If you don't, they will build up inside of you and you will end up pregnant. Or at the very least, bloated.*

<u>SOME SUGGESTIONS:</u>

- Boss people around. Start sentences with, "While you're under my roof," even if they are not.

- Remind friends to bring a sweater.

- Get yourself a dad bod (fun fact: anyone can have a gut. It's non-gender specific).

- Help a friend with their work project. Then send them to bed and stay up all night finishing it.

- Lick your thumb and rub the smudge off your friend's face.

- When the walk sign lights up at a crosswalk, say to the random person next to you, "Hold my hand."

- Learn to swaddle your poodle.

- Use your spoon as an imaginary airplane/
train/Aston Martin.

- Hold your neighbor's hair when they
barf.

- Tuck your partner in at night.

- Relearn algebra.

- Hand someone 20 bucks and say, "Don't
spend it all in one place."

- Tell a friend you'll pick them up from the
mall and forget to show up.

- Get an ice cream with a friend. Using your
tongue, push their scoop down securely into
their cone to keep it from falling off.

- Spend your summer touring college
campuses.

- Donate $108,584 to a university in your
state. (The average cost of attendance for
a student living on campus at an in-state
public 4-year institution.)

- Donate $182,832 to a university *out*-of-
state.

- Donate $234,512 to a private university.

# Spell out words to keep secrets.

# CHAPTER 13

# HOW TO PROVE YOU'RE AN ADULT (EVEN THOUGH YOU DON'T HAVE KIDS)

Some say you aren't truly an adult until you become a parent. We say true dat.

But there are some ways you can mask your immaturity and fool the masses:

- Drink scotch without ice.

*It's adult 'cuz it's burny in my tum-tum!*

- Set the table with the "good" china.

- Buy some good china.

- Use words like: portfolio, codicil, vichyssoise, cassoulet, onomatopoeia, duffifie. Bonus points for using three or more in a sentence. Bonus points if you know what duffifie is.

- Say things like, "When I was your age, I walked to school in the snow, uphill, both ways." And, "Money doesn't grow on trees."

- Shop in bulk.

- Keep your pets up to date on all their vaccinations.

- Get your prostate checked and get mammograms regularly.

- Complain about the cost of groceries, electricity, and prescriptions.

- Talk about the Nasdaq.

- Put a Baby on Board sticker on your car.

- Pay someone to do stuff for you.

- Watch documentaries.

- Make friends with wine and cheese shop
  owners.

- Send a sympathy card when someone
  dies.

- Create a living will and trust. Leave
  everything to your favorite charity. 'Cause
  you're dead. And you don't have anyone to
  leave stuff to. Whoa. That just got dark.

# PREPARING FOR OLD AGE

Who will take care of you in your sunset times?

This is a legitimate fear, my friends, along with, "Who will take care of my tortoise when I die?" and "To whom will I leave my antique doll collection?"

Use the following ideas to plan for care in your twilight. (Not the vampire kind, sorry.)

- Bribe your niblings (nieces and nephews) *now* to care for you *later*.

- Make friends with people at least 20 years younger than you. Bonus if you chose ones with no corrective lens requirements on their drivers' licenses.

- Fashion yourself a Golden Girls commune. Find 3 of your lady friends to cohabitate. Wear house dresses, tease each other relentlessly, and solve all disputes with sarcasm and cheesecake.

- Recreate the Odd Couple - this one's for the guys. Find your most opposite friend and cohabitate. Never compromise, roll your eyes at each other frequently, and avoid all talk of feelings.

- And if you outlive all your friends, there's always "The Retirement Community For Wayward, Slutty Old Persons." Trust us, they're out there. Lots of STDs! But hey, at least you're too old to accidentally get pregnant!

NEVER TOO LATE TO GET THE CLAP!

# DAILY AFFIRMATIONS FOR THE CHILDFREE

Choose to feel great about your childfree self with affirmations. Don't forget thoughts become words, words become actions, actions become hamsters, hamsters become ... oh crap, lost our train of thought.

Repeat the following affirmations every morning. In your head. Or out loud in public. Do this every day for 66 days and see how your life transforms!

# **<u>AFFIRMATIONS</u>**

I am a woman of many cats.

I feel free to take a bath for 3 hours straight.

My life has meaning and endless opportunities for
sex on the kitchen counter.

I am becoming all that I am destined to be, starting
with this doobie.

I feel good about all my earthly possessions being
buried with me. Just like the Pharaohs.

I am Mother to those of my own choosing.

I feel compassion and love for
the mothers around me.

I am free to walk away whenever I want.

My responsibilities are first to me
and second to myself.

Not my baby, not my problem.

I forgive myself for not using my uterus
the way God intended.

I have a choice, even though my body
tried to make the choice for me.

I feel confident and whole about my choice, even if
others don't.

I radiate prosperity and peace of mind about my
choice to be childfree.

I radiate health and rest
because I got up at noon.

I am my own child. I am my own child.
I am my own child.

Money flows to me effortlessly.
And I get to keep it all.

I am strong. I am independent.
I am alone. And I like it.

My body belongs to me.
Parasites are not welcome here.

I see myself in my *own* eyes.

Love is a river that flows through me.
And then back to me.

Everything is working out. For me. Just me.

I am so in love with myself there is
no room for anyone else.

I am
grateful
for me. I
love me.
Me me me.

# CHAPTER 16

# NEXT STEPS

Now that you've got all the NOT MOMS know-how, *now what?*

Brunch? A trip to Paris? Go back to bed?

We've found that being childfree is the most fun when you can share your adventures with other like-minded adults. If all your current friends have kids, don't worry! You can make new friends – friends without kids. We did and now look at us! We wrote a book together about our mutual experiences. You know, the one you're reading right now.

So go! Go find the people who get you.

All it takes to make friends without kids is to be incredibly forward and rude and ask someone if they plan to never ever have children, forsaking all parenting dreams 'til death.

Using this undignified approach has allowed us to meet more and more people who have chosen the childfree life. Occasionally, we do lose one or two to the evils … oops, we mean, "enchantments" of parenthood. But then we just go to the Cat Cafe and pick up a few more.

No Cat Cafes in your town? Start one! Or even better, start your own NOT MOMS meet-up group!

Too afraid to venture out into the world? Want to stay in your peaceful cocoon? No problem! We have a solution for that, too. Join our private Facebook group for fellow NOT MOMS! And follow us on Instagram.

TIKTOK: @not.moms

INSTAGRAM: @notmoms

FACEBOOK (Private Group): NOT MOMS

Share the joys and frustrations of being childfree. Brag about what you do with your free time. Commiserate about how the world doesn't always accept your decision and how that sometimes makes you feel disregarded and sad. Hooray! JOIN US! JOIN US! JOIN US! Seriously, you should join us. We get you.

Now go! Get outta here! We have nothing left to teach you. Plus, we need to sleep. Our friend's baby is sleeping.

# OTHER UNFINISHED WORKS BY THESE AUTHORS

F*CK KIDS! (Nope. That's a terrible title. And that's why we don't have kids.)

KIDS SUCK! (Wait. That's a terrible title too. And another reason why we don't have kids.)

MY MOM TALKS ABOUT HER 48-HOUR LABOR: AN UNAUTHORIZED BIOGRAPHY

HOW TO STILL BANG! AND OTHER THINGS YOU CAN DO WHEN YOU DON'T HAVE KIDS!

I LOVE YOU TOO MUCH TO HAVE YOUR KIDS

I DON'T HAVE KIDS. THEREFORE I AM.

I CHOOSE ME. THE LITTLE SELFISH BOOK OF STICK IT TO THE MAN.

YOUR MOM DOESN'T WANT YOU TO HAVE KIDS EITHER

(OTHER UNFINISHED WORKS CONT.)

YOU WEREN'T MEANT TO HAVE KIDS

FOOTLOOSE AND CHILDFREE

SOMETIMES LIFE IS BETTER ALONE!

PROCREATION IS FOR THE BIRDS AND BUNNIES!

And!

Testy the Bunny says:
Leave the procreation
to us bunnies!

# YOUR CHILDFREE JOURNEY

Use the following prompts to help document your childfree journey.

Your descendants ... er ... the future members of your family tree (with your branch having no offshoots) will enjoy reading about your history.

From your big decisions to the mini milestones, here is a place for you to record the meaningful moments of your childfree life to celebrate and tell your story to your — anyone who will listen — for years to come.

1.  **How I told my significant other that I don't want kids:**

_______________________________________

_______________________________________

_______________________________________

_______________________________________

_______________________________________

_______________________________________

_______________________________________

2.  **How I told my family I am not having children:**

_______________________________________

_______________________________________

_______________________________________

_______________________________________

_______________________________________

_______________________________________

3.  **How I told my LYFT driver and gynecologist that I am not having children:**

________________________________________________________

________________________________________________________

________________________________________________________

________________________________________________________

________________________________________________________

________________________________________________________

________________________________________________________

4.  **Stupid things people have said about my choice to not have kids:**

________________________________________________________

________________________________________________________

________________________________________________________

________________________________________________________

________________________________________________________

________________________________________________________

________________________________________________________

5.  **Comments my family and friends have made after I told them I was not going to have kids:**

_________________________________________

_________________________________________

_________________________________________

_________________________________________

_________________________________________

_________________________________________

_________________________________________

6.  **I love to frivolously spend my extra money on:**

_________________________________________

_________________________________________

_________________________________________

_________________________________________

_________________________________________

_________________________________________

_________________________________________

7. **Things my friends with kids have done that led me to my decision to not have kids:**

_______________________________________

_______________________________________

_______________________________________

_______________________________________

_______________________________________

_______________________________________

_______________________________________

_______________________________________

8. **Things I've heard or seen between couples that led me to the decision to not have kids:**

_______________________________________

_______________________________________

_______________________________________

_______________________________________

_______________________________________

_______________________________________

_______________________________________

_______________________________________

9.  **Early inciting incidents that led me to not wanting kids:**

_____________________________________________

_____________________________________________

_____________________________________________

_____________________________________________

_____________________________________________

_____________________________________________

_____________________________________________

_____________________________________________

10. **Things I am afraid of because of my choice to not have children:**

_____________________________________________

_____________________________________________

_____________________________________________

_____________________________________________

_____________________________________________

_____________________________________________

## 11. When did I make the final decision to not have children?

__________________________________________________

__________________________________________________

__________________________________________________

__________________________________________________

__________________________________________________

__________________________________________________

__________________________________________________

## 12. In my free time, my favorite things to do are:

__________________________________________________

__________________________________________________

__________________________________________________

__________________________________________________

__________________________________________________

**13. Fun things I have done on the spur of the moment because I don't have kids:**

_______________________________________

_______________________________________

_______________________________________

_______________________________________

_______________________________________

_______________________________________

_______________________________________

_______________________________________

**14. My brilliant friends who also have made the choice to be childfree:**

_______________________________________

_______________________________________

_______________________________________

_______________________________________

_______________________________________

_______________________________________

_______________________________________

_______________________________________

## 15. My non-human children are:

_______________________________________

_______________________________________

_______________________________________

_______________________________________

_______________________________________

_______________________________________

_______________________________________

## 16. My cat's favorite toys are:

_______________________________________

_______________________________________

_______________________________________

_______________________________________

_______________________________________

_______________________________________

_______________________________________

_______________________________________

## 17. My cat's favorite foods are:

## 18. Sharp things and other child unfriendly items in my house:

**19. People in my life who act like children that I parent:**

_______________________________________

_______________________________________

_______________________________________

_______________________________________

_______________________________________

_______________________________________

_______________________________________

_______________________________________

**20. Ways that my partner behaves like a child, which inadvertently give me the feelings of being a parent, which inadvertently make me glad I'm not a parent:**

_______________________________________

_______________________________________

_______________________________________

_______________________________________

_______________________________________

_______________________________________

## 21. Things I do to prove I'm an adult even though I don't have kids:

## 22. Things I like to do in my home while naked:

## 23. Things I don't have to hide in my house because they are child unfriendly:

_____________________________________________

_____________________________________________

_____________________________________________

_____________________________________________

_____________________________________________

_____________________________________________

_____________________________________________

_____________________________________________

## 24. My Sleeping patterns:

_____________________________________________

_____________________________________________

_____________________________________________

_____________________________________________

_____________________________________________

_____________________________________________

_____________________________________________

# 25. Places I've traveled:

## 26. My own ridiculous answers to the question, "why are you not having kids?"

Formula: We both love (insert favorite weird thing) and we don't want to pass that trait down.

Formula: We like to (insert seedy thing you like to do) and we don't want to stop.

Formula: We can't, we own a (insert thing that is dangerous to kids).

________________________________________

________________________________________

________________________________________

________________________________________

________________________________________

________________________________________

________________________________________

________________________________________

________________________________________

________________________________________

________________________________________

________________________________________

# MORE ABOUT KATIE & JULIE

Friends KATIE VON TILL and JULIE WITTNER are NOT MOMS in real life, but have played hundreds of moms on TV, film, commercials, and the stage. Having pretend kids is hard. Having real kids is WAY harder. So Katie and Julie are sticking with the pretend ones.

With their simpatico life choices and similar comedic voices, Katie and Julie began writing together in 2016. They wrote a television pilot, a short film, and now this book. Writing this together has been a celebration of all the long sessions where they would share grievances, belly laughs and ethical conversations about the choice to have or not to have kids.

Follow them on:

TikTok: @not.moms

Instagram: @notmoms @katievontill @juliewittner

# ABOUT MATT

MATTHEW PATRICK DAVIS is also a NOT MOM in real life (at the present moment), but did play The Mother in a horror movie called Barbarian, so he knows a thing or two about bottle-feeding (spoiler alert). In addition to playing scary ladies, he also writes kids' songs for Disney and Disney Jr. shows, because those two things totally make sense together. Why not throw  in being an illustrator? He is grateful to Katie and Julie for giving him an excuse to pick up a pencil (well, Apple Pencil) and draw again, adding one more spinning plate to this polymath's arsenal of disparate career paths.

Follow him on Instagram: @matthewpatrickdavis